THE CULTURAL REVOLUTION

Years of Chaos in China

by Andrew Langley

THE CULTURAL REVOLUTION

Years of Chaos in China

by Andrew Langley

Content Adviser: Kevin G. Cai, Ph.D., Assistant Professor of Asia Pacific Studies, Renison College, University of Waterloo

Reading Adviser: Susan Kesselring, M.A., Literacy Educator, Rosemount-Apple Valley-Eagan (Minnesota) School District

Compass Point Books ✦ Minneapolis, Minnesota

COMPASS POINT BOOKS

3109 West 50th Street, #115
Minneapolis, MN 55410

For Compass Point Books
Brenda Haugen, XNR Productions, Inc., Catherine Neitge,
Keith Griffin, Lori Bye, and Nick Healy

Produced by White-Thomson Publishing Ltd.

For White-Thomson Publishing
Stephen White-Thomson, Susan Crean, Amy Sparks,
Tinstar Design Ltd., Kevin G. Cai, Peggy Bresnick Kendler,
Brian Fitzgerald, Barbara Bakowski, and Timothy Griffin

Library of Congress Cataloging-in-Publication Data
Langley, Andrew.
 The Cultural Revolution : years of chaos in China / by Andrew Langley.
     p. cm. — (Snapshots in history)
 Includes bibliographical references and index.
 ISBN 978-0-7565-3483-7 (library binding)
 1. China—History—Cultural Revolution, 1966-1976—Juvenile
literature. I. Title. II. Series.
 DS778.7.L36 2008
 951.05′6—dc22   2007032699

Visit Compass Point Books on the Internet at
www.compasspointbooks.com
or e-mail your request to
custserv@compasspointbooks.com

CONTENTS

Mao and Mass Hysteria

It was early morning on August 18, 1966, and still dark. Yet the center of Beijing, China's capital city, was buzzing with activity. More than 1 million young people were on the march. Schoolchildren, college students, and workers tramped through the streets, singing, chanting, and shouting. They had come to see their country's leader, Chairman Mao Tse-tung, known simply as Mao to them and the world. Many thousands of them had just arrived, packed in trains from all over China. Thousands more were from Beijing itself.

The young people, mostly teenagers, called themselves Red Guards. They were devoted followers of the leader and had organized themselves into sections to promote his policies. In the summer of 1966, Mao had sent a message

Students marched through Tiananmen Square in Beijing carrying placards in support of Chairman Mao Tse-tung.

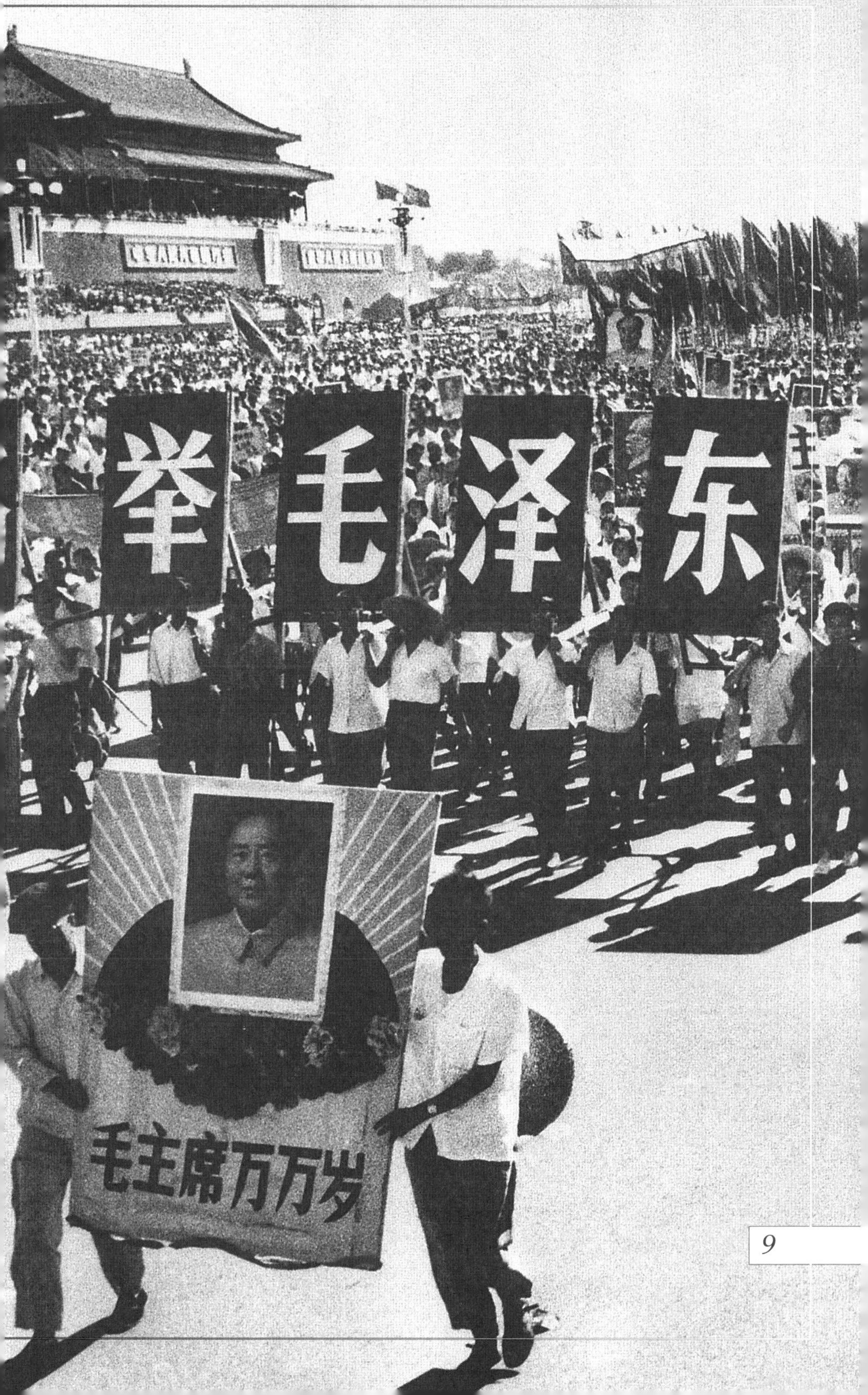
举
毛
泽
东
毛主席万万岁

to all young people warning that the ideas behind the Chinese Revolution were in danger. He encouraged them to physically attack all Chinese people whom they believed were betraying its communist ideals. He said that these "traitors" included teachers and even Communist Party officials.

Following Mao's message, Red Guard groups sprang into action and brought terror to many towns in China. The violence was especially severe in Beijing. High school students tortured teachers by tearing their clothes, pouring ink on them, scalding them with boiling water, and beating them with nail-spiked clubs. Many of the victims were badly injured, and several committed suicide. All schools and universities closed down.

August 18, 1966, marked the beginning of a series of giant Red Guard rallies in Tiananmen Square. There would be eight in all in the following weeks, attended by nearly 9 million young people. For most of them, it was a life-changing experience. One Red Guard who saw

THE CHINESE REVOLUTION

Communism is an economic and political system of governing a country that was developed by German philosopher Karl Marx and others during the 1800s. It is based on the state ownership of property and the sharing of resources evenly among the inhabitants. Marx believed this would happen only when workers seized control and toppled the traditional rulers in a revolution. Russia became the world's first communist country after a revolution in October 1917. The Communist Revolution in China did not succeed until 1949, when the Chinese Communist Party, led by Mao Tse-tung, gained power after a long civil war.

Mao at a rally described the thrill of the occasion
in a letter:

*Let me tell you great news, greater than
heaven! I saw our most dearly beloved leader
Chairman Mao! Today I am so happy my heart
is about to burst! I have decided to make today
my birthday! Today I started a new life!*

*Mao Tse-tung was
greatly admired by the
young Red Guards
who attended the
August 18, 1966, rally
in Tiananmen Square.*

Mao Tse-tung reviewed the Red Guard forces from where he stood at the Tiananmen Gate on August 18, 1966.

Red Guards, most of whom were 12 to 17 years old, came to the capital in force, summoned by Chairman Mao. They all headed for a single destination: the vast open space of Tiananmen Square.

On August 18, since just after midnight, the square had been filling up with hordes of young people. As dawn broke, the noise and excitement grew. The crowds saw that Mao himself had appeared high atop the Tiananmen Gate at the side of the square. He was wearing the uniform of the People's Liberation Army, the main wing of the Chinese armed forces. Next to him stood other leaders, including the smaller figure of Lin Biao, the minister of defense and Mao's close colleague.

The Red Guards were almost hysterical. They chanted "Long live Chairman Mao!" and "10,000 years to Chairman Mao!" They sang hymns in praise of the Chinese Revolution and its leader. They marched in battalions past the gate, where Mao and Lin smiled and waved.

After several hours, Mao came down and walked among the crowds. Carefully protected by bodyguards, he shook hands and chatted with many of the students. The chanting grew even more deafening, and people surged forward to get a close-up glimpse of their leader.

The biggest thrill of all was reserved for a specially selected group of students who were taken to meet Mao and China's other leaders. It was also a shock for them. When they got close to 72-year-old Chairman Mao, he looked his age. His hair was going white, many of his teeth were black, and he moved slowly. His army uniform was slightly too small and made him look pudgy.

Many Red Guards were thrilled to talk with Mao and shake his hand during the Tiananmen Square rallies.

Even so, nothing could spoil the feeling of ecstasy. One of the young female students, Song Binbin, presented Mao with a Red Guard armband. He allowed her to put it on his arm, to show that the Guards had his approval. When the girl told him

her name, which means "gentle and polite," Mao replied it would be better to "be warlike." Song Binbin immediately changed her name to Yao Wu, which means "Be warlike."

Next Lin Biao made a speech to the massive crowd below. He urged the Red Guards to search out and destroy all the "old ideas, old culture, old customs, and old habits of the exploiting classes." These were soon known as the "Four Olds." They stood as targets of the new movement that Mao and his colleagues created, which had already let loose a wave of violence against the old ways. The movement was to become the Chinese Cultural Revolution, and during the next three years it would bring chaos and bloodshed to the whole country—and shock the rest of the world.

Who Was Mao Tse-tung?

Mao Tse-tung was born the son of a rich peasant in central China on December 26, 1893. He helped found the Chinese Communist Party in 1921 and became a legend when he led communist forces against the invading Japanese in 1937. By 1949, he had won power from China's ruling Nationalist Party, and he became leader of the People's Republic of China. Cunning, ruthless, and utterly determined, Mao turned his country into a tightly controlled communist society.

The Creation of Communist China

In the early 1900s, China was considered by Western nations to be a feeble and backward country. Ruled by emperors for more than 2,000 years, China had hardly developed since the Middle Ages. The vast majority of the population lived in poor peasant villages, where they barely managed to grow enough food to eat. Western nations, including the United States, France, and Great Britain, controlled its seaports and most foreign trade.

The last Chinese emperor gave up his throne in February 1912, and China became a republic governed by the Nationalist Party. But within two years, the new nationalist government had fallen apart, and there was no strong ruler. By 1916, the country was split by civil wars among local warlords.

In the early 1900s, the majority of Chinese people were poor peasants who lived in rural areas of the country.

During this time, much of Chinese public life was based on Confucian thought. Confucius was the most famous and important Chinese philosopher. He had lived about 2,400 years before. His teachings stressed the need for correct

The philosopher Confucius was born in about 551 B.C.

behavior, which included being just, sincere, kind, loyal, and well mannered. He believed that people should develop their sense of morality and personal duty.

In the midst of the chaos in the country in the early 1900s, a tiny seed of hope was planted. In June 1921, the first meeting of the Chinese Communist Party took place in Shanghai. Just 13 people attended the meeting, but during the next two decades the party would grow into the most popular and powerful force in China.

Mao Tse-tung was at that first meeting, and he quickly became a leading figure in the Communist Party. The key to the party's early success was in its appeal to vast numbers of rural peasants. The party organized peasant armies, encouraged rebellion, and built up a network of local communist governments in rural areas of the country. It also built the communist Red Army, made up of local warriors and bandits, refugees, and political recruits.

The Communist Party faced huge obstacles in building a following. The nationalists were trying to reunite the country, and they launched a series of savage attacks through the late 1920s and early 1930s. They killed thousands of communists.

THE NATIONALIST PARTY

The Chinese Nationalist Party was formed in 1912 from revolutionary groups that had overthrown the last emperor. Nationalists formed China's first democratic government but were soon forced from office. From then on, nationalist armies led by Chiang Kai-shek tried to regain control of the country, fighting local warlords, Japanese troops, and the communists. After his final defeat in 1949, Chiang moved to the island of Taiwan.

In 1934, the remains of the communist Red Army were forced to flee across China to take refuge in the remote north. This "Long March" became a legend and made Mao and his followers into heroes.

A brutal Japanese invasion of China in July 1937 spelled even greater danger

THE JAPANESE INVASION

In 1931, Japanese troops occupied Manchuria in northeastern China. The nationalists were not strong enough to fight them. In 1937, the Japanese launched a full-scale invasion of central China. Japanese forces took over all major cities in China, sometimes behaving with great cruelty. In Nanjing, more than 300,000 Chinese people were killed. The Japanese withdrew only after their country was forced to surrender to Allied forces in 1945 at the end of World War II.

than the chaos of civil war. The nationalists were driven back by the Japanese, but the communists had by now recovered their strength. They resisted the Japanese with guerrilla tactics such as ambushes and hit-and-run attacks rather than major battles. Their success made them even more popular.

Japan entered World War II after its attack on U.S. Navy ships at Pearl Harbor in Hawaii on December 7, 1941. At the same time, China joined the United States, Great Britain, and other countries that were fighting on the Allied side against the Axis Powers, which included Japan, Germany, and Italy. Both communists and nationalists received assistance from the Allies and combined their forces to fight the Japanese. However, the communist forces had much greater success than the weakened and unpopular nationalists.

Once the war was over, fighting between communists and nationalists in China broke out again. This time, however, the communists had a much bigger army, which rapidly gained control of major cities, including Tianjin and Beijing. The victorious communists proclaimed the founding of the People's Republic of China on October 1, 1949.

The U.S. government supplied Chinese communists with machine guns and other weapons to fight the Japanese.

21

MAO'S COLLEAGUES

Although Mao took the lead in 1949, he was supported by other important figures, who would have a big impact in years to come:

Liu Shaoqi
The second most powerful leader, he was seen as the likely successor to Mao.

Chou En-lai
Popular and charming, Chou became premier and was in charge of the day-to-day running of the country.

Lin Biao
A brilliant battlefield commander during the 1940s, he would play a major role in the Cultural Revolution.

China was now ruled by the Central People's Government Council, which had been elected by Communist Party members. Mao was chairman of this ruling council and the most powerful person in the land. The revolution had triumphed, and it was time to transform China into a communist society. Mao and other communists condemned Confucius for being elitist. Communism would change the very fabric of Chinese public life—and its future.

The first step was to rebuild the economy—which was shattered after decades of civil and international war—starting with agriculture. For centuries, poor peasants had owned little land. The peasants had rented plots for farming from rich landlords, who made up only 10 percent of the population yet owned nearly half of all farmland.

Mao started a campaign to take farmland away from the landlords and share it with the peasants. He sent teams of volunteers to villages to organize this land reform. They held mass meetings where peasants could talk about the wrongs they had suffered from the landlords. The process often led to violence. Many landlords not only lost their land but also risked being beaten and even put to death.

Poor farmers denounced landowners during the land reforms that came after the Chinese Revolution of 1949.

The period of 1949 to 1953 was one of growing bloodshed throughout China. The communists hunted down anyone thought to be opposed to the ideas set forth during the revolution. These "counterrevolutionaries" were arrested and sentenced in mass trials all across the country. Historians believe that at least 2 million people died in this wave of terror.

In 1953, China launched its first Five-Year Plan, a strict program designed to boost the economy. The plan encouraged the growth of heavy industry, such as steelmaking and engineering. All major industries were brought under the control of the government.

However, economic progress was slow, and many people in China were not happy with the state of the country. Land reforms did little to make peasants' lives any easier. Industry was growing quickly, but it was often inefficient and poorly managed. Severe food shortages occurred.

Some leaders might have decided to take a more cautious approach and plan to change things more gradually.

CHINA AND THE SOVIET UNION

The Soviet Union was a group of communist countries, including Russia, which lasted from 1922 until 1991. It was the leader of the communist world in the 1920s and strongly supported the Chinese Communist Party in its early years. After 1949, the Soviet Union sent arms and money to help establish the People's Republic of China. However, during the 1950s, Mao criticized the Soviets for not being warlike enough toward Western countries. In 1963, he broke off relations altogether, and the flow of Soviet aid dried up.

Mao did the opposite. He decided to push things along even faster, hoping for a huge explosion of growth. "Our nation is like an atom," he said. "When this atom's nucleus is smashed, the thermal energy released will have really tremendous power."

China's second Five-Year Plan, which began in 1958, was known as the Great Leap Forward. Mao was determined to reorganize rural China through this plan. Ancient farms and villages were lumped together into giant communes, or collective farms. Everybody had to work for the benefit of the communes instead of themselves.

One of the main aims of the Great Leap Forward was to double the production of steel within a single year. To achieve that goal, the government ordered that small furnaces be set up in every commune. Pots, tools, and other household items were melted down. Peasants were taken away from farmwork so they could tend the furnaces.

The project was a failure. The backyard furnaces could produce only low-quality iron instead of steel, so efforts and materials were wasted. This disaster was echoed in other aspects of the Great Leap Forward. Peasants were forced to use new seed-sowing methods and new plows, which did not work. Because of these changes and a lack of farm laborers—who were operating the furnaces—poor harvests resulted in 1958.

The situation grew much worse during the next three years because of bad weather. A terrible famine ravaged the country, and a horrifying number of peasants starved to death. One survivor remembered:

> *My legs and hands were swollen and I felt that at any moment I would die. Instead of walking, I crawled and rolled to save energy. I peeled off the bark of a locust tree and cooked it as if it were rice soup.*

In desperation, some villagers became so hungry they even began eating their own children. Hundreds of cases of cannibalism were later reported in Anhui and Gansu provinces. Altogether, historians calculate, between 15 million and 30 million peasants died in the famine from 1959 to 1962.

Millions of Chinese children starved to death during the Great Leap Forward.

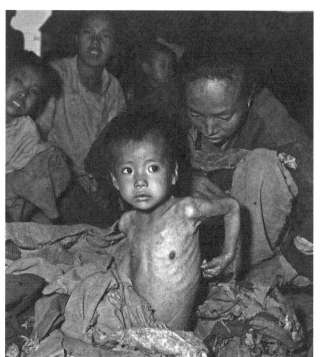

The Great Leap Forward turned out to be a catastrophe, but Mao and his supporters could not admit this. Mao did not like being proven wrong about anything. A few leading communists were critical of the program, but they were quickly removed from power. However, the crisis still led to a growing split in the Communist Party.

The split damaged Mao's authority. Although he remained party chairman, he retired as China's head of state in 1959 and appeared less often in public. The new president was Liu Shaoqi, who introduced more moderate policies. He reversed many of the plans for the Great Leap Forward. Big collective farms were broken up, and peasants were allowed to move back to their smaller plots of land. More money was spent on farm machinery.

Slowly, the economy began to heal. By the mid-1960s, China's production levels of grain and other foods had been restored to earlier levels. Industry was growing at a faster rate, and even the population was rising again. The nightmare seemed to be over.

"Great Disorder Under Heaven"

Chapter

3

A fter he stepped down as leader, Mao became increasingly unhappy with the state of the People's Republic of China. He believed that the communist leaders were not being revolutionary enough. They were simply trying to make the country peaceful and prosperous, rather than building a dynamic communist state. Mao thought they had forgotten about the great ideals they had once shared.

Mao wanted a more violent kind of revolution in which the masses took direct action to change old ways. Again and again he had preached that communism was all about struggle. "Poor people want change, want to do things, want revolution," he had said in 1958. He urged the Chinese to fight for a new way of life, with slogans such as "Never forget class struggle."

As he grew older, Chairman Mao faced other worries. When he was 71 years old, he started to fear that rivals might push him into retirement. He had been deeply shocked in October 1964 when the Soviet leader Nikita Khrushchev was toppled from power after a plot by his colleagues. Mao feared that the same fate might be waiting for him.

Mao was still a great hero to the Chinese people. His supporters had built up a "cult of personality," which had turned him into a godlike figure who watched over all aspects of daily life. There were pictures of Mao all across the country on giant

Posters of Mao appeared all over China during the 1960s to promote the "cult of personality."

posters and celebrations of his deeds in school textbooks. Millions of copies of *Quotations from Chairman Mao Tse-tung*, a collection of his ideas, had been published. There was even a popular saying that started with these words: "Father is close, mother is close, but neither is as close as Chairman Mao."

Mao decided to take back control of China and return the country to a revolutionary course. He would go on the attack. First he would get rid of the Communist Party officials whom he felt were going back to the old ways of capitalism. He made speeches calling these people "capitalist roaders" and "revisionists," or those who made changes to the original ideas of Marxism.

Liu Shaoqi was seen as the successor to Chairman Mao until Mao turned against him in the mid-1960s.

Mao's most obvious target was Liu Shaoqi, who was re-elected as president of China in January 1965. Liu was building up a strong power base and planning to cut back Mao's influence.

Mao began to criticize Liu in speeches, but he could not challenge him openly yet. Instead he verbally attacked other "moderates" whom he saw as Liu's allies. Two of Mao's closest supporters helped him in his attacks—Lin Biao, a veteran of the civil war who was minister of defense, and Mao's fourth wife, Jiang Qing.

Their first notable victim was Luo Ruiqing, the chief of the People's Liberation Army, who was seen as a revisionist and a threat to communist ideals. At a Communist Party meeting in Shanghai in late 1965, Mao's supporters criticized Luo harshly, and soon he was facing opposition on all sides. In despair, he tried—and failed—to kill himself by jumping from a three-story building. Mao's response was "How pathetic!"

The purge, or clearing out, of Communist Party officials carried on into the early months of 1966. But Mao wanted to enlarge his campaign and make it go faster. His next step would shock the world and cause an even bigger upheaval in China than the Great Leap Forward had done.

Mao had often been hostile toward intellectuals, a group that included everyone from playwrights and artists to teachers and journalists. He saw them as part of the old, elitist culture that belonged to an arrogant middle class and excluded

JIANG QING

When she was a young woman, Jiang Qing was a successful stage and film actress. She joined the Communist Party in 1936 and married Mao in 1939. Ambitious, ruthless, and a fiery speaker, she played a major part in the Cultural Revolution. In 1969 she joined the Politburo, the main ruling body of the Chinese Communist Party.

ordinary people. He now planned to get rid of them by launching a new kind of revolution—the Cultural Revolution.

In May 1966, the Politburo issued a document that mentioned the Great Cultural Revolution for the first time. Soon after this, Jiang Qing helped set up the Cultural Revolution Group. Lin Biao continued to boost Mao's image. In a speech at this time, he said: "Chairman Mao is a genius; everything the Chairman says is truly great; one of the Chairman's words will override the meaning of 10,000 of ours."

Jiang Qing, Mao's fourth wife, was a powerful figure in China's Communist Party.

The revolution was soon in full swing. On May 25, 1966, young lecturers at Beijing University put up a poster attacking the university president and other teachers. The lecturers accused the other teachers of being revisionists who were betraying the Cultural Revolution. The lecturers called for stronger leadership at the university. The poster caused outrage on the campus. Within hours, students had hung hundreds of revolutionary posters.

BIG-CHARACTER POSTERS

The *dazibao*, or "big-character" poster, had been used in China for many years but became popular in the Maoist era. The poster—a large sheet of paper with handwritten script—was stuck up on a wall in a public place. It might contain a message, an announcement, or a political slogan. Because big-character posters could be put up in secret, they were seen as protests against governments that suppressed free speech.

Mao was delighted. Mao had always believed that young people made the best revolutionaries. He also believed that the revolution should be a violent and massive one. He told Jiang Qing that he wanted to create "great disorder under heaven." The focus of that disorder, he hoped, would be the schools and universities of China, where students would defy their teachers. One group of students published a set of proposals in the *People's Daily* newspaper. The proposals called for revolutionary change to the curriculum and methods of teaching, which should be based on Mao's ideas.

A few days after the first poster went up at Beijing University, Mao ordered Chinese newspapers and radio stations to publish its words. This showed that he approved of what the students had done. The rebellion against teachers spread rapidly, and thousands of posters appeared in schools and universities throughout China. One said:

> *Since we want rebellion, the matter has been taken out of your hands! We are going to make the air thick with the pungent smell of explosives!*

Students in Beijing created political posters attacking party officials.

Soon the education system in most Chinese cities shut down. Many school directors were dismissed from their posts. But simply writing posters was not enough for some students. They were determined to criticize and punish anyone they saw as an enemy of Mao. This led to horrific acts of violence. In Nanjing, a teacher found students tearing pages from a book:

> *She was pushed to the floor. One girl picked up a torn-out page. "Eat!" she shouted, and pushed the paper into the face of the teacher. "Eat it!" She forced the page into the mouth of the teacher, and made her chew it, urged on by a few slaps across the face. Then one of the boys punched her.*

As the chaos and brutality increased, Liu Shaoqi tried to take action. He sent 400 work teams of loyal Communist Party members into the schools and universities to prevent the worst of the violence. This made him unpopular with young people, and it also made Mao's position stronger.

At that time, Mao was not even in Beijing. He had been away in the north, leaving his supporters to direct the beginnings of the Cultural Revolution. He decided to reappear in public in July 1966. He caused a sensation by joining competitors in a swimming event in the Yangtze River.

Mao then returned to Beijing and took charge of the government immediately. He ordered Liu to withdraw the work teams from the universities

Chairman Mao's swim in the Yangtze River on July 16, 1966, was intended to show that he was still strong and healthy.

and insisted that it was wrong to suppress the student movement.

Mao promised to support a new group of revolutionary students who were calling themselves Red Guards (red was the color of communist revolution). The Red Guards, aged 12 to 30,

COMMUNIST PARTY STRUCTURE DURING THE CULTURAL REVOLUTION

Standing Committee
Made up of four to five members, it included the party chairman and the state president.

Politburo
The main ruling body, it included 12 to 15 members.

Central Committee
Made up of 200 to 300 members, it met frequently throughout the year.

Party Congress
It included delegates from regional committees and met only once every five years.

Regional party organizations
They led the work within each individual region.

organized themselves into sections and detachments and set up headquarters at the provincial and municipal levels. They elected leaders who were constantly subject to recall.

Mao even put up his own poster on the door of the Central Committee room. It urged the Red Guards to attack the Communist Party leaders: "Bombard the headquarters!"

The Red Terror

On August 8, 1966, the Central Committee of the Chinese Communist Party approved a document called The 16 Points. Inspired by Mao, it called for even greater efforts to push forward the Cultural Revolution. New mass campaigns were to be organized. Anyone who opposed revolution or believed in old ideas and habits would be criticized and purged.

The 16 Points were broadcast on national radio that night. Recordings of the text and speeches by Lin Biao and Chinese Premier Chou En-lai went on sale in stores. People—especially the young—were urged to study them and put them to use.

The young Red Guards were enthralled with their new power. For centuries, the Chinese had revered older people for their experience and wisdom. Young people were expected to obey

In the summer of 1966, as Mao and his supporters advanced the Cultural Revolution, more and more young people joined the Red Guard and took to the streets.

and respect their parents and elders. Even after the 1949 revolution, power had stayed in the hands of the older generation.

THE 16 POINTS

1. This is a new stage in the socialist revolution.

2. The revolution has a main current, but sometimes twists and turns are necessary.

3. Be bold and daring to arouse the masses.

4. Trust the masses and let them educate themselves.

5. Rely on the revolutionary left and strike at the counter-revolutionaries of the right.

6. People are bound to hold different views. These should be debated in a reasonable way.

7. Be on guard against those who call the masses "counterrevolutionaries."

8. Most cadres [trained officials] are good socialists, but all antiparty rightists must be exposed.

9. New cultural revolutionary groups, committees, and congresses are very important.

10. There must be educational reform.

11. "Bourgeois" and "reactionary" people should be criticized by name.

12. Special care should be taken of scientists as long as they are not against the party and socialism.

13. The socialist education movement should be integrated in city and countryside.

14. Take firm hold of the revolution and encourage production.

15. The cultural revolution should be carried out in the armed forces.

16. Mao Tse-tung's thought is the guide to action in the great proletarian cultural revolution.

Now Mao encouraged young people to attack the whole framework of Chinese politics and society. He and Lin Biao told them that the "Four Olds"—old thought, old culture, old customs, and old habits—were to be smashed and destroyed.

The Red Guards saw themselves as an army building a new China. They wore green military uniforms with red armbands and carried copies of *Quotations from Chairman Mao Tse-tung*. In this book Mao had written: "You young people, full of vigor and vitality, are in the bloom of life. Our hope is placed on you. The world belongs to you."

THE LITTLE RED BOOK

Quotations from Chairman Mao Tse-tung is a collection of more than 400 excerpts from Mao's writings and sayings. It was first published in China in 1964, and since then more than 900 million copies have been printed. The pocket edition, known in the West as *The Little Red Book*, was produced because every Chinese person was expected to have one and be able to quote from it. During the Cultural Revolution, each student and worker had to carry a copy.

The first of the great Red Guard rallies in Tiananmen Square came on August 18. Mao had decreed that young people should be able to travel anywhere at no cost and be given free accommodations during the coming months. This ensured that there were huge crowds in Beijing. Red Guards also traveled to other parts of China, spreading the news of the Cultural Revolution.

The campaign became more savage and destructive. Red Guard factions tore through towns and cities looking for people they suspected of being counterrevolutionaries, class enemies, or capitalist roaders. Red Guards plastered walls with posters criticizing the suspects and held mass meetings to denounce and sometimes torture them.

Driven on by the propaganda of Jiang Qing and the Cultural Revolution Group, Red Guards often humiliated their victims at the mass meetings. The Red Guards beat and kicked the people, tore their clothes, covered them with ink, shaved their heads, and forced them to wear pointed caps. The Red Guards twisted their victims' arms behind them and forced them to bend forward in what was called the "jet-plane" position. The Red Guards hung placards around

Red Guards traveled to the town of Ningxia to prompt the people living there to destroy the "Four Olds."

their victims' necks describing what they had done wrong. All the time, the Red Guards shouted accusations and insults.

Often the victims were innocent of any anti-Maoist acts. Many were chosen for punishment simply because they were in positions of authority. Doctors, lawyers, librarians, local leaders, and others were automatically seen as "bourgeois reactionaries" who thought themselves superior to the masses. Others, such as teachers and university professors, were sometimes chosen out of spite and revenge by students who had received poor grades.

Scenes of terrifying violence took place in most parts of China. Many people were horrified by what they saw. Jung Chang's father, who was a civil servant, was repeatedly beaten and shouted at. Jung recalled:

> *I saw him standing on a slow-moving truck, being paraded through the streets. A huge placard hung from a thin wire that was eating into his neck, and his arms were twisted ferociously behind his back.*

Eventually, her father went mad. Her mother suffered almost as badly. She was brutally beaten by fellow workers at a factory and was forced to kneel on broken glass and wear a dunce's cap.

The Red Guards took their battle against the "Four Olds" into houses, museums, and workplaces. They burst into people's homes and stole or smashed

43

anything they deemed too old or too intellectual. Books, musical instruments, paintings, jewelry, Western-style clothes, furniture, and ornaments were all looted. The Red Guards ransacked museums and ancient Buddhist temples and burned or otherwise destroyed beautiful statues. They also beat up monks and attendants.

The death toll mounted as the chaos spread. Hundreds of people committed suicide after such treatment, and thousands more were killed by the mobs. In August and September 1966, there were 1,772 murders in Beijing alone. Nobody was ever arrested or tried for these crimes.

By this time, Liu Shaoqi was no longer the leader of China. Mao had taken away his power and replaced him with Lin Biao. Lin was now seen as Mao's deputy and likely successor. Liu, on the other hand, was forced to criticize himself and was soon placed under house arrest in Beijing.

The chaos caused by the Cultural Revolution had shut down factories, schools, and many other institutions. But Lin Biao and Jiang Qing wanted to create even more mayhem. In January 1967, they launched the "January Storm" in Shanghai. They encouraged a huge force of radical workers to overthrow the Communist Party leaders of the city and set up their own Maoist government there.

This purging of local party leaders quickly spread to other towns and districts across the country. It also struck at the central government in Beijing. Revolutionaries seized power in most of the ministries, including the important Foreign Ministry, which dealt with relationships with other countries. Most of China's ambassadors abroad were summoned home.

The Communist Party banned many books during the Cultural Revolution. Red Guards burned the books in big piles.

In fact, the Cultural Revolution had resulted in a major breakdown of law and order. Many different sets of people were struggling for power—students, workers, soldiers, peasants, and Communist Party cadres, or trained officials. Even the Red Guards had split up into dozens of different factions, all with their own aims and slogans. The different factions denounced one another and often fought bloody street battles.

Purging quickly spread to all parts of China. The cities of Beijing, Shanghai, and Yinchuan were all hit by violence.

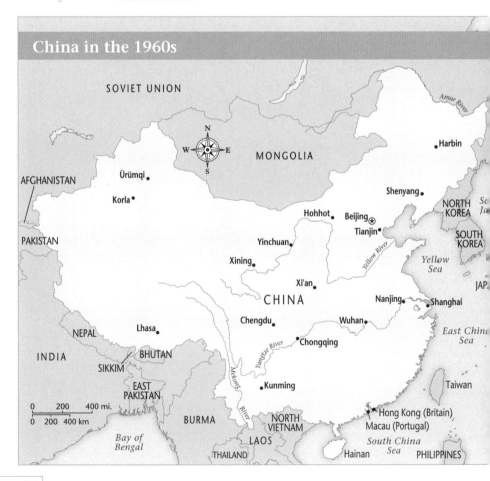

China in the 1960s

The only organization keeping order was the People's Liberation Army (PLA), the main military force of the People's Republic of China. But in July 1967, most of its power was taken away. Mao asked, "Why can't we arm the workers and students?" Jiang Qing announced that the Red Guards would replace the PLA when needed. This allowed the Red Guards to seize weapons and ammunition from army barracks, which they could use to fight each other. Mao's Cultural Revolution was out of control. ◣

TROUBLE ABROAD

The upheaval of the Cultural Revolution and the actions of the Red Guards shocked many foreign governments and caused trouble in other countries. In early 1967, there were fights between Chinese students and police in the Soviet Union, and the Chinese Embassy in Moscow was damaged. French and Indian diplomats were attacked in Beijing, and the British Mission there was destroyed by fire. By September, China had quarreled with more than 30 foreign countries.

Restoring Order

By September 1967, Mao had realized that his Cultural Revolution was in danger of becoming a civil war. In many parts of China, different factions and rebel groups were fighting one another. There were fierce battles and hundreds of deaths. The situation was especially bad in Sichuan, the province at the center of the arms industry in China. Fighters stole tanks, field guns, and armored cars from factories.

The danger grew even clearer to Mao when moderate rebel factions seized control of the city of Wuhan. Mao came to the city in person with soldiers and called on the rebel leaders to resign, but they refused. Demonstrators took to the streets, protesting against Mao's policies. Worst of all, they broke into the grounds of his nearby luxury villa and threatened his staff.

Red Guards in Guangzhou demonstrated against the Four Olds at about the same time that factions within the Red Guards started fighting against one another.

ECONOMIC DECLINE

The chaos of the Cultural Revolution in China closed not only schools and universities but factories, mines, and foundries. The result was a decline in most areas of industry, making the country much poorer. Figures for 1967 show the decreases:

Industry	Decline
Steel production	30 percent
Coal production	18 percent
Construction	30 percent
Oil production	23 percent
Goods imported	12 percent

A year earlier, Mao had praised students and other revolutionaries and given them the freedom to rebel, criticize, and destroy. Now that policy looked like a terrible mistake, which had led to a breakdown of law and order. Mao did not admit his mistake publicly, though. He suddenly turned against the Red Guards. "They are politically immature," he said. "We can't trust them with things of major importance. They embrace the bourgeois world outlook."

He gave instructions to the Politburo that the situation must be brought under control. Chou En-lai made a speech ordering the Red Guards to stop the fighting and to give back the arms they had looted. Lin told PLA troops that they now had the right to fire on all rebels. He also recruited armed bands of workers, who were used to subdue the warring factions.

Chou and Jiang Qing launched a new campaign to "sort out class ranks." This was yet another purge of the Chinese Communist Party. It was aimed at any member who was thought to be a threat to

Chou En-lai called on the Red Guards to stop fighting one another.

51

party unity. Thousands of ordinary communists throughout China were expelled or killed. Chou was now able to begin the long task of forming new local committees in the provinces that would be faithful to Mao.

To back up this message, there was a fresh surge in the promotion of Mao as a cult figure. Classes in "Mao Tse-tung Thought" were set up across the country. By early 1968, the Great Leader was being praised in daily morning rituals everywhere. People stood in front of a portrait of Mao, sang songs about

MAO QUOTATIONS FOR EVERYONE

Selected quotations from Mao Tse-tung's works were set out for use in everyday life in China. People were expected to know the correct reply to each phrase:

Worker 1: *"Vigorously grasp revolution ..."*	Worker 2: *"... energetically promote production!"*
Peasant 1: *"Self-reliance ..."*	Peasant 2: *"... ample food and clothing!"*
Student 1: *"Study well ..."*	Student 2: *"... make progress every day!"*
Cadre 1: *"Keep in step with Chairman Mao ..."*	Cadre 2: *"... never cease to make revolution!"*
Soldier 1: *"The army and the people ..."*	Soldier 2: *"... united like one!"*
Old person 1: *"Let us respectfully wish Chairman Mao eternal life without end ..."*	Old person 2: *"... eternal life without end! Eternal life without end!"*

him, and held up *The Little Red Book*. Then they listened to readings from Mao's books before they set off for work.

Slowly the rebel factions and "class enemies" were savagely suppressed. In Guangxi province, for example, the PLA and worker gangs beat to death an estimated 3,680 people during a 10-day period of violence. In Inner Mongolia, more

Children in Red Guard uniforms read from The Little Red Book *in front of a giant poster of Mao Tse-tung.*

53

than 1 million people were imprisoned or executed in 1968. The brutal campaign brought the situation back under control.

Mao's next step was to bring peace to the universities and schools. In July 1968, more than 30,000 Beijing factory workers were formed into work teams. They were sent to school campuses to restore order. Liu had tried to use work teams back in 1966, and Mao had condemned him for it. Now Mao was copying Liu's idea.

THE DEATH OF LIU SHAOQI

During 1967, the campaig against Liu Shaoqi, China's forme president, grew stronger. The PL. arrested anybody connected wit him, including his son. Liu and hi wife were mocked and criticize at mass meetings. In Octobe 1968, Liu was expelled from th Communist Party and held alon in prison. His wife was charge with spying for the United State and also imprisoned. Liu die a year later, after a long an painful illness during which h was refused medicines. He wa cremated, and Mao ordered tha his death be kept a secret. Liu ashes were not handed over t his wife until 1980.

Some students tried to fight the teams with stones and bullets, but in the end they were forced to give in. The power of the Red Guards had been broken. But they might still cause trouble if they stayed on campuses. Mao decided the best plan was to send them far away. Mao launched the "Down to the Countryside Movement" in December 1968. He gave orders that students and other educated young people from the cities should travel into the country and live and work in villages and on farms. The party directive that gave the order stated:

Graduates must become ordinary peasants or ordinary workers. Put public interest first, submit to the needs of the state, and go to the countryside and factories and mines, where the conditions are the hardest.

Peasants recited passages from Mao's Little Red Book *every day before they started work in the fields.*

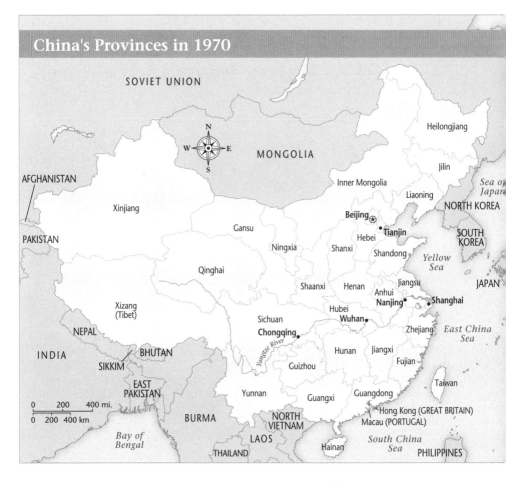

China's Provinces in 1970

Students were sent to the outermost provinces of China as part of the Down to the Countryside Movement.

During the next seven years, at least 12 million young people, many of them teenagers, were sent to live in peasant communities, often in distant settlements. They had to stay there for periods lasting between six months and three years, though many stayed much longer than that and were unable to return home. The work could be hard, since farming methods had not changed for hundreds of years. Anhua Gao was one of the students ordered to spread manure on the rice fields. She described her early experiences:

> *Surrounded by millions of flies, we stood in water that came halfway up our legs and trampled the muck down into the mud with our feet. It was dirty, stinking and slippery. What was even worse was discovering the first leech. When I raised my leg, a dozen of the disgusting things were clinging to me.*

The luckier students were sent to work in provinces near their homes or to richer areas near the big cities. Many others had to spend days traveling to remote regions near the Chinese border in the far north, such as Inner Mongolia or Xinjiang.

The northern border was also the setting for a new clash between China and the Soviet Union. Relations between the two countries had been poor for several years. Mao thought the Soviet leaders had become "revisionist" and had forgotten the true ideals of communism. At the start of the Cultural Revolution, the Soviet army had moved large numbers of soldiers to its border with China.

Early in 1969, Chinese troops ambushed a Soviet force on a river island on the northeast border, killing several soldiers. Mao had planned this attack as a way to show the strength of the Chinese armed forces, but he was not expecting such a strong reaction from the Soviet Union. The Soviets were outraged. They called in more troops and tanks and began firing shells and missiles into China. Alarmed, Mao told the Foreign Ministry to begin peace talks with the Soviet Union.

COMMUNIST PARTY CONGRESS

The Congress is a meeting of delegates who represent all the members of the Communist Party throughout China. At a Congress, between 1,000 and 1,500 delegates gather in the Great Hall of the People in Beijing. The Congress lasts for about 10 days, during which the delegates elect the party's Central Committee and approve the policies of the party leadership. There is little debate, because all the important decisions are made beforehand by the party leaders. There is no set interval between Congress meetings. There was a gap of 13 years between the 8th Congress (1956) and the 9th Congress (1969).

In April 1969, the Chinese Communist Party held its 9th Congress in Beijing. Lin Biao was one of the first people to speak. He praised Mao and "Mao Tse-tung Thought" and criticized Liu Shaoqi. Then Chou En-lai made a speech praising Lin Biao. It was no surprise when Lin was named as Mao's "close comrade-in-arms and successor."

Mao also used the Congress to announce the formal end of the Cultural Revolution. But he hinted that the fight against class enemies and revisionists would continue. He said, "The job of the Great Cultural Revolution is not yet finished." This was true. Many historians believe that the Cultural Revolution continued in China for several years. They date the real end of it much later— to Mao's death in 1976 and the arrest of others involved at the highest levels.

In spite of the peace talks, Chinese leaders also took the chance to inflame delegates' feelings

against the Soviet Union. Chou called for people to unite against the enemy. He quoted Mao when he said, "Faced with a formidable foe, we had better get mobilized [prepare for war]."

Some historians believe that by fueling anger toward the Soviet Union, Mao and his followers were distracting others from the problems caused by the Cultural Revolution. ◣

Chairman Mao (left) and Lin Biao appeared together at the 9th Communist Party Congress in Beijing in April 1969.

The Fall of Lin Biao

Chapter

6

Following the 9th Congress, Lin Biao was at the height of his power. He had been officially named as Mao's successor and the next leader of the People's Republic of China.

But almost as soon as Lin hit his peak, his power base began to shrink. He was head of the army, which had grown strong again thanks to its part in crushing the rebel factions. However, that strength was slipping away once more as the Communist Party was reorganized and local committees began to take control.

Another danger came from Mao Tse-tung. By the end of 1970, Mao would be 77 years old and close to retiring. Despite his age, he was still energetic and determined to stay in charge. He grew angry at any challenge to his authority. He had already destroyed one major rival for the

Mao (right) saw Lin Biao as his successor but became jealous when Lin's power base grew too strong.

leadership—Liu Shaoqi. Would he turn against Lin Biao in the same way?

Since Liu's dismissal, no one had replaced him as president of the People's Republic of China. Many members of the Politburo had urged Mao to take the post again, but he had refused. He said:

> *I, Mao Tse-tung, do not want to be chairman. If the committee decides to maintain such a position, it is Lin Biao who should hold the position.*

At the Communist Party's Central Committee meeting in August 1970, Lin tried once more to persuade Mao to become chairman. In his speech, he praised Mao as a genius and said that without

China's Central Committee met frequently throughout the year.

him the Communists would not have gained their victories.

Mao was not flattered by these words. In fact, he behaved as if he were angry—and suspicious of Lin's actions. Although Mao had declared that Lin should be chairman, Mao now suspected a more cunning plot. He believed that Lin wanted to be named the deputy chairman. This meant that Lin would not openly challenge Mao but would become leader if Mao retired or died.

Mao believed that Lin was preparing to take over from him. Mao began a series of actions to weaken Lin's position. He dismissed Lin's allies in the Central Committee. He arrested senior PLA officers who supported Lin and replaced them with his own followers.

Lin quickly realized that he was under threat and remembered the terrible fate of Liu Shaoqi. Lin began to plan ways to escape by leaving China altogether and flying across the border to the Soviet Union. At the beginning of 1971, he also withdrew from public life, refusing to appear at Communist Party conferences and parades.

Nobody knows exactly what happened after this. The official Chinese accounts claim that Lin's son, whose nickname was "Tiger," was plotting against Mao. They said he had formed a secret group that condemned Mao's leadership, calling Mao "the biggest feudal tyrant in Chinese history." The group is said to have discussed the possibility of assassinating Mao by attacking his special train with flamethrowers, rockets, and guns. Many modern historians question these accounts.

However, there is no doubt about what happened in the end. On the night of September 13, 1971, Lin Biao, his wife, and his son took off in an aircraft and headed for the Soviet border. A few hours later the aircraft crashed in Mongolia, killing everyone on board. Nobody knows what caused the crash.

The Chinese Politburo tried to keep the tragedy quiet, but news slowly filtered out. Senior party members immediately began to condemn Lin as a traitor to the revolution. Ordinary people were shocked by the story. Even Mao became ill and depressed. His personal doctor recorded: "He took to his bed and lay there all day, saying and doing little."

The death of Lin Biao left Mao with plenty of problems. The first was, who would be his successor? Lin was disgraced and dead. Many of his closest colleagues were aging, ill, or in disgrace. Chou En-lai was suffering from cancer. In September 1972, Mao brought in a young party leader named Wang Hongwen to work for the government in Beijing. Wang seemed to be the new favorite.

Mao was feeling old and less energetic. He was, in fact, in the early stages of a disease that would

Following the death of Lin Biao, young people held a performance criticizing his attempt to take power from Mao.

After the chaos of the Cultural Revolution, Chinese workers prepared to deliver a record grain harvest. Premier Chou En-lai's reforms resulted in record harvests in 1971 and again in 1973.

destroy the nerves in his throat, chest, and limbs. He was happy to leave the daily running of affairs to the loyal Chou En-lai, who had been China's premier since 1949. Chou's deputy was Deng Xiaoping, who had been purged in the early days of the Cultural Revolution but had now returned to power.

Hardworking and levelheaded, Chou pushed on with plans to develop China's economy. These plans had been laid down in the Five-Year Plan that began in 1971. With Chou's moderate and sensible approach, things began to improve. Industrial and farming output rose steadily. By 1975, the grain harvest finally got back to levels that had not been reached since the Great Leap Forward of 1958.

Other areas of life started to recover from the horrors of the late 1960s. Schools and universities reopened and returned to the previous ways of teaching. China's relations with foreign countries continued to progress. China even became friendlier with neighboring Japan for the first time since World War II. The growing openness meant that China could bring in foreign factories and technology from the United States, Japan, and Europe. ◣

A New Era

Chapter 7

After the official end of the Cultural Revolution, China's relations with the outside world continued to improve. Soviet troops were gathering on the Chinese border, but they would not cross it unless China attacked first. A new Soviet ambassador had arrived in Beijing in late 1970—a sign that the situation had calmed.

China was also building new links with the United States and other Western countries. This effort was a major change of policy. Since 1949, hostility had existed between the capitalist United States and communist China. The Chinese and Americans had supported different sides in several conflicts in Asia. The most recent of these was in Vietnam, on China's southern border, where huge numbers of U.S. troops had been fighting.

The United States and China were on opposite sides of the war in Vietnam.

In 1969, the United States government slowly started withdrawing its troops from Vietnam. This meant that another threat to China's borders was disappearing. The Americans noted that inside China the fever of the Cultural Revolution was beginning to cool down. Both Mao and U.S. President Richard Nixon were ready to improve relations between the two nations.

The first moves were simple ones. The U.S. government lifted some restrictions on travel and trade with China. In April 1971, the Chinese government invited the U.S. table tennis team to play friendly matches in China in what was called "ping-pong diplomacy." In July 1971, Nixon's adviser Henry Kissinger flew to Beijing for secret talks with Chou En-lai.

This was just the beginning. A week later, it was announced that Nixon himself would visit China—the first U.S. president to do so. In October 1971, the United Nations—an organization of representatives from different countries that promotes international peace and understanding—

THE VIETNAM WAR

In the late 1950s, guerrilla armies backed by the communist government of North Vietnam invaded South Vietnam. The conflict grew into an international war. The United States and other Western countries supported South Vietnam with troops and arms, while China and the Soviet Union supported North Vietnam. By 1969, more than 500,000 U.S. troops were fighting in Vietnam. But it was clear that the war could not be won, and the Americans began a withdrawal that was completed in 1975. More than 2 million Vietnamese and 57,000 Americans died in the war.

voted to admit the People's Republic of China as a member. It took the place of the Republic of China, which was based in Taiwan. China had cut itself off from the world during the Cultural Revolution. Now it was opening up again.

China became a member of the United Nations in 1971.

71

President Nixon arrived in China on February 21, 1972. He spent the week visiting famous sites such as the Great Wall and Tiananmen Square and talking for many hours with Chou En-lai. Nixon was one of the first world leaders to make contact with the

President Richard M. Nixon and his wife, Pat, visited China in 1972.

Chinese government after the isolation of the Cultural Revolution period. However, his meeting with Mao lasted barely an hour, and Mao refused to discuss politics.

The tour had few practical results. Nixon agreed to supply the Chinese with American goods, including chemicals, trucks, building equipment, and car engines. But Mao offered little in return. He still wanted other communist leaders to see him as an opponent of the United States. Even so, the visit opened up communication between the two giant countries after decades of silence. Nixon said afterward, "This was the week that changed the world."

It appeared that China was becoming more prosperous and peaceful. But all was not well. Chou En-lai's moderate policies were very different from Mao's vision of a great Cultural Revolution in which the masses seized power and smashed bourgeois thinking and capitalist roaders. Maoist radicals, led by Jiang Qing, were outraged at the way that Chou was softening Mao's revolutionary thought. On top of this, Chou was seriously ill. In 1972, doctors told him that he was suffering from bladder cancer. He spent long periods in the hospital. Deng Xiaoping performed more of the daily tasks in running the government.

THE PEOPLE'S REPUBLIC OF CHINA

The People's Republic of China is geographically the third–biggest country in the world, after Russia and Canada. It has the largest population, with about one-fifth of the world's people. Huge areas of the country are mountain or desert, and the vast majority of the people are crammed into China's eastern regions.

73

In the summer of 1973, radicals launched a new campaign called "Criticize Lin, Criticize Confucius." This was partly a new round of condemnation of Lin Biao and partly an attack on Chou himself. Jiang and her radical team could not criticize the premier by name, so they used a substitute target—the ancient Chinese philosopher Confucius. It was clear, however, that their words were aimed at Chou.

Four people who later became known as the Gang of Four headed the radical group. They included Mao's wife, Jiang Qing, and the man many people believed would be Mao's successor, Wang Hongwen. Even so, Mao did not give them his full support. When they told him Chou and Deng were plotting against him, Mao took no notice.

WANG HONGWEN

Wang Hongwen worked as a security guard in a cotton factory in Shanghai. He joined the Red Guards in 1966 and quickly became a leading rebel against Liu Shaoqi. He was a close colleague of Jiang Qing and was appointed to the communist Central Committee in 1969. Many thought he would succeed Mao as Chinese leader in the early 1970s. Wang was the youngest member of the Gang of Four.

Maoist radicals, led by the Gang of Four, were a serious threat to China's development. They called for more revolution and less prosperity. "To stop production is revolution itself," ran one slogan attacking industrial output. "We would rather have socialist weeds than capitalist crops," said another about agriculture. As for education, Jiang's team said, "We want illiterate working people, not educated spiritual aristocrats."

The radical movement, however, was not a success—probably because most people were tired of the violence and destruction that had marked the Cultural Revolution. In late 1974, the Gang of Four ended the campaign, though they remained fiercely critical of the policies of Chou and Deng.

By the middle of 1975, illness was taking a stronger grip on Chairman Mao. He went into the hospital for eye treatment, but doctors could do little about his worsening infections and disease. Chou's health was also growing worse. The Gang of Four took the opportunity to launch new attacks on Deng, with slogans like "The Capitalist Roaders Are on the Move!"

Chou En-lai died on January 8, 1976. His death shocked millions of people throughout China. One woman remembered the fear she felt when she heard the radio announcement:

> At that moment I could see no future for China. Premier Chou had been the last barrier between we ordinary Chinese and the excesses of Mao's wife and her thugs.

On April 4, a traditional Chinese holiday called Qingming, thousands of Beijing citizens assembled in Tiananmen Square to pay their last respects to Chou. Most of them laid wreaths in piles that reached as high as a house. Many also attached poems and statements. Some included messages attacking the Gang of Four and even Chairman Mao himself.

The government was alarmed. The next morning trucks were sent to take away the wreaths. Citizens were outraged and flocked back to the square. The crowd quickly grew to more than 2 million people, and some fought with police or set fire to cars. The gathering had turned into a mass protest meeting. That evening, PLA troops cleared the area, beating up and dragging away the last demonstrators.

Deng was blamed for the incident and was stripped of all his power. It looked as though the Gang of Four had gained a victory and gotten rid of its main enemy. However, the new premier was Hua Guofeng, a moderate like Chou and Deng. Hua was a long-serving communist official who did not support the aims of the radicals. Plus, the gang was about to lose its protector. Although Mao had never officially supported the Gang of Four, he had encouraged them behind the scenes.

Mao Tse-tung died just after midnight on September 9, 1976. There was a long period of mourning, and many public rallies commemorated the dead leader. But many people were not sad to see him go. "I felt elation [joy] rise up in me," Anhua Gao wrote in a memoir many years later. Another young woman, Jung Chang, wrote in her autobiography, "The news filled me with such euphoria [joy] that for an instant I was numb."

It was the end of an era. Mao had been a major figure in China since the Long March of 1936, and

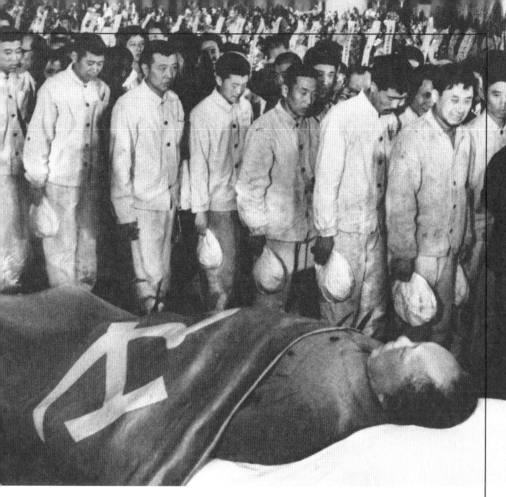

he had been the country's real leader since 1949. Mao was the single most important person in the creation of the People's Republic of China. His last great project had been the Cultural Revolution, and it ended with his death. ◣

In 1976, thousands came to Beijing to pay their last respects to Mao after his death.

China After Mao

The Cultural Revolution and many other programs Mao launched during his 27 years in power did not improve the quality of life in China. In fact, they did a great deal to damage it. Even the work of Chou En-lai had only restored the 1970s economy to the level of the 1950s. In the country, peasants struggled to get enough food and fuel. In the cities, housing and services were bad, and unemployment was rising.

Once Mao was gone, the new premier, Hua Guofeng, moved quickly to get rid of Mao's closest supporters. On October 6, 1976, Hua ordered the arrest of the Gang of Four. They were expelled from the Communist Party and later imprisoned. The government took the opportunity to blame Jiang Qing and

her colleagues for the horrors of the Cultural Revolution. They could not blame Mao, because he was still a godlike figure.

Jiang Qing (left) was sentenced to death at the trial of the Gang of Four in 1981, but this sentence was later changed to life imprisonment.

The fall of the Gang of Four was greeted with joy in most parts of China. Anhua Gao remembered:

> *China was one big party as the people celebrated. Because now they had hope. Firecrackers exploded everywhere. The noise was deafening. A stranger might have thought that China had been liberated from a foreign invader instead of just five Chinese people. Because, no matter what the leaders said, we thought of the Gang of Four as really a Gang of Five, headed by Mao.*

The country now needed reform and stability. Hua was not a strong enough leader, and in 1977 Deng Xiaoping was brought back from exile to be his deputy. Soon Deng announced that China could make progress only by turning away from Maoism. "We must reject flashiness without substance and every sort of boasting," he said. "There must be less empty talk and more hard work."

DENG XIAOPING

Deng Xiaoping was an early supporter of Mao. He took part in the Long March and led military campaigns. As a colleague of Liu Shaoqi, he quickly fell from power at the beginning of the Cultural Revolution and was sent to work in a remote tractor factory. But he was brought back into politics by Chou En-lai and became vice premier in 1974. Deng was a prime target of the Gang of Four and was purged once more in 1976—though his career was not yet over.

Chinese society had been deeply wounded by the Cultural Revolution, and the wounds needed time to heal. For example, countless thousands of victims had been denounced during the Cultural Revolution and sent to prison or into exile. Now these people returned to their old homes and jobs. Many found it difficult to live and work next to those who had accused and imprisoned them.

Hua resigned as premier in 1980, and Deng became the leading figure in China for the next 10 years. He opened the country wider to the outside world, aiming to attract goods and investment money from foreign countries. He believed this was the best way to expand industry and trade and make the country wealthier. Deng also reformed agriculture by allowing farmers to sell their surplus crops, a practice that had been forbidden under Mao.

But economic growth was not enough on its own. As China developed, people wanted greater freedom in how they behaved and a bigger say in how their lives were governed. By the late 1980s, young people were demanding more civil rights, such as the right to vote for their rulers, better education, and action against official corruption.

British Prime Minister Margaret Thatcher met Deng Xiaoping in Beijing in 1982.

Once again Tiananmen Square in Beijing was the setting for a massive rally. In June 1989, more than 100,000 students and workers gathered peacefully, defying police orders to disperse. Communist Party leaders sent troops with tanks and machine guns to break up the rally. At least 2,000 unarmed demonstrators were killed, and many more were injured or arrested.

The tragedy in Tiananmen Square shocked the world. It also showed ordinary Chinese people that

the Communist Party would continue to keep a strong grip on law and order and stamp down on freedom of expression—just as it had since 1949.

Through the 1990s, however, the tensions slowly eased. Deng, the last of the old revolutionaries, died in 1997 and was replaced by younger leaders with more modern ideas. Industry and trade began to grow at great speed. Today China is the fastest-developing nation in the world, with an economy thought to be worth $2 trillion.

During the night of June 3, 1989, PLA troops opened fire on student demonstrators in Tiananmen Square, killing many people.

83

Less than 30 years since the end of the Cultural Revolution, the turnaround is an astonishing transformation. It has brought with it great riches, as well as small improvements in personal freedoms. These include access to Western-style goods, such as clothing and fast food, and the opportunity to run independent businesses. Some historians believe that the rapid growth is a direct result of the end of the Cultural Revolution.

Beijing has become one of the fastest-growing cities in the world.

The mass rallies, the cult of Mao, the brutality of the Red Guards, the fighting between factions, the bloody purging of capitalist roaders, and the

frenzied campaigns were all part of a national nightmare. They showed that radical Maoism would not work. Instead of bringing equality, strength, and a just society, they brought chaos, hatred, and poverty.

When the Cultural Revolution ended, Deng and other leaders knew that China had to take a different path. It had to follow the example of successful Asian nations such as Japan and South Korea and build up an economy based on Western capitalist values. This policy has turned China into one of the world's economic superpowers.

China remains a strict communist state. Many people believe and hope that in the near future it will become a democracy where citizens can speak their true thoughts and elect their own government. Only then, they say, will it be free from the oppression and fear it has faced so many times since the Cultural Revolution began. ◣

Timeline

▶ **January 1, 1912**

The Republic of China is founded.

▶ **February 12, 1912**

China's last emperor leaves
the throne.

▶ **July 23, 1921**

The Chinese Communist Party
is founded.

▶ **August 14, 1945**

World War II ends; Japan surrenders
and withdraws from China; civil war
breaks out between nationalists and
communists in China.

▶ **October 1, 1949**

Mao Tse-tung proclaims
the People's Republic of
China in Beijing.

▶ **1953**

China's first Five-Year Plan for the
economy begins.

▶ **May 1958**

The second Five-Year Plan, the Great
Leap Forward, is launched.

▶ **1959**

Mao retires as
head of state; he
is succeeded by
Liu Shaoqi.

▶ **1959–1962**

Famine, largely caused by the Great
Leap Forward, kills 15 million to
30 million people.

▶ **May 1966**

Politburo document announces
"Great Cultural Revolution;"
Cultural Revolution Group is
established; first political posters
appear at Beijing University.

▶ **June 1966**

Wave of violence begins against
teachers in major cities.

▶ **August 29, 1966**

Mao pledges
support for Red
Guards; he writes
his own dazibao
slogan, "Bombard
the Headquarters;"
Chinese
Communist Party
publishes "The
16 Points."

▶ **August 16–November 26, 1966**

At least 11 million people attend
series of eight Red Guard rallies
in Beijing.

▶ **January 3, 1967**

Red Guards seize power in Shanghai
during the "January Storm."

July 1967

Liu Shaoqi and his wife are publicly denounced; People's Liberation Army (PLA) is banned from action against Red Guards; uprising spreads to major cities.

September 1967

Rebel factions take over the city of Wuhan.

July 1968

Work teams restore order on campuses.

October 1968

Liu is expelled from the Communist Party.

December 1968

"Down to the Countryside Movement" begins as thousands of students and cadres are sent to villages and farms.

March 1969

Military clashes occur on the Soviet border.

April 1, 1969

Lin Biao is named Mao's successor.

November 12, 1969

Liu Shaoqi dies.

September 13, 1971

Lin Biao dies in a plane crash in Mongolia.

October 1971

China becomes a member of the United Nations.

February 1972

U.S. President Richard M. Nixon visits China.

April 1973

Deng Xiaoping is named deputy premier.

January 8, 1976

Chou En-lai dies.

April 1976

Hua Guofeng becomes new premier; mass demonstration against the Gang of Four occurs in Tiananmen Square.

September 9, 1976

Mao Tse-tung dies.

October 6, 1976

Arrest of the Gang of Four.

Timeline

▶ *1977*

Deng returns as deputy premier.

▶ *1980*

Hua Guofeng resigns; Deng becomes leader of China.

▶ *June 1989*

 Student demonstration in Tiananmen Square ends in massacre by PLA troops.

▶ *February 19, 1997*

Deng Xiaoping dies.

ON THE WEB

For more information on this topic, use FactHound.

1 Go to *www.facthound.com*

2 Type in this book ID: 0756534836

3 Click on the *Fetch It* button. FactHound will find the best Web sites for you.

HISTORIC SITES

Chinese American Museum
El Pueblo de Los Angeles
125 Paseo de la Plaza, Suite 400
Los Angeles, CA 90012
213/485-8567
www.camla.org

The museum explores the history of Chinese Americans through exhibits and educational programs.

LOOK FOR MORE BOOKS IN THIS SERIES

A complete list of **Snapshots in History** titles is available on our Web site: *www.compasspointbooks.com*

Glossary

bombard
to attack with missiles or blows

bourgeois
having attitudes and behavior marked by conformity to the standards of the middle class; belonging to the property-owning class

capitalist roader
politician who is moving toward a capitalist outlook

collective farm
state-controlled farm made up of several smaller farms

commune
collective units in rural areas with governmental, political, and economic functions; also known as people's commune

counterrevolutionary
someone who works against a revolution

cult of personality
building up of great admiration and worship for an individual person

dazibao
a poster, usually handwritten in big characters, making a comment on current events

elitist
belonging to, or favoring, a select group of people

guerrillas
soldiers who are not part of a country's regular army and who fight using small, surprise attacks rather than large battles

nationalist
someone who has a strong sense of nationalism; used specifically to refer to soldiers and members of the Chinese Nationalist Party

People's Liberation Army (PLA)
the armed forces of the People's Republic of China

Politburo
group of 19 to 25 people who hold central control of the Chinese Communist Party (short for Political Bureau)

premier
the chief or prime minister of a country

proletarian
part of the working class

purge
removal of all one's opponents or possible enemies by force

radical
extreme in comparison to what most people think or do

republic
political system in which officials are elected to represent citizens in government

revisionist
someone who tries to rewrite communist theory to justify a retreat from the revolutionary position

socialism
economic system in which the government owns most businesses

Source Notes

Chapter 1

Page 11, line 3: Rana Mitter. *A Bitter Revolution: China's Struggle with the Modern World.* New York: Oxford University Press, 2004, p. 221.

Page 13, line 12: Roderick MacFarquhar and Michael Schoenhals. *Mao's Last Revolution.* Cambridge, Mass.: Belknap, 2006, p. 107.

Page 15, lines 1 and 3: Anhua Gao. *To the Edge of the Sky.* New York: Penguin Putnam, 2000, p. 147.

Page 15, line 10: *Mao's Last Revolution*, p. 108.

Chapter 2

Page 25, line 3: Craig Dietrich. *People's China: A Brief History.* New York: Oxford University Press, 1994, p. 121.

Page 26, line 6: *A Bitter Revolution: China's Struggle with the Modern World*, p. 197.

Chapter 3

Page 28, line 13: *Mao's Last Revolution*, p. 1.

Page 28, line 16: *People's China: A Brief History*, pp. 156, 157.

Page 30, line 5: Jung Chang and Jon Halliday. *Mao: The Unknown Story.* London: Jonathan Cape, 2005, p. 507.

Page 31, line 19: *Mao's Last Revolution*, p. 27.

Page 32, line 9: "China—The Cultural Revolution." *h2g2.* 26 October 2005. 26 August 2007. www.bbc.co.uk/dna/h2g2/A5141369

Page 33, line 19: *Mao's Last Revolution*, p. 52.

Page 34, line 4: *People's China: A Brief History*, p. 182.

Page 35, line 9: *To the Edge of the Sky*, p. 146.

Page 37, line 8: *People's China: A Brief History*, p. 184.

Chapter 4

Page 41, line 15: *Mao's Last Revolution*, p. 107.

Page 43, line 18: Jung Chang. *Wild Swans: Three Daughters of China.* New York: Simon & Schuster, 1991, p. 464.

Page 47, line 7: *Mao's Last Revolution*, p. 215.

Chapter 5

Page 50, line 7: *People's China: A Brief History*, p. 195.

Page 51, line 4: *Mao: The Unknown Story*, p. 566.

Page 52, sidebar: *Mao's Last Revolution*, p. 266.

Page 55, line 1: Ibid., p. 251.

Source Notes

Page 57, line 1: *To the Edge of the Sky*, p. 217.

Page 58, line 6: *People's China: A Brief History*, p. 206.

Page 58, line 11: *Mao's Last Revolution,* p. 285.

Page 59, line 3: Ibid., p. 312.

Chapter 6
Page 62, line 8: Ibid., p. 326.

Page 64, line 13: *Mao: The Unknown Story*, p. 578.

Page 64, line 30: *Mao's Last Revolution*, p. 339.

Chapter 7
Page 73, line 16: Jeremy Isaacs and Taylor Downning. *Cold War.* London: Bantam Press, 1998, p. 278.

Page 74, line 26: *Wild Swans: Three Daughters of China*, p. 618.

Page 75, line 13: *Mao's Last Revolution*, p. 410.

Page 75, line 19: *To the Edge of the Sky*, p. 276.

Page 76, line 24: Ibid., p. 290.

Page 76, line 27: *Wild Swans: Three Daughters of China*, p. 658.

Chapter 8
Page 79, line 6: *To the Edge of the Sky*, p. 292.

Page 80, line 11: *People's China: A Brief History*, p. 240.

SELECT BIBLIOGRAPHY

Jung Chang and Jon Halliday. *Mao: The Unknown Story*. London: Jonathan Cape, 2005.

Dietrich, Craig. *People's China: A Brief History*. New York: Oxford University Press, 1994.

Anhua Gao. *To the Edge of the Sky*. New York: Penguin Putnam, 2000.

MacFarquhar, Roderick, and Michael Schoenhals. *Mao's Last Revolution*. Cambridge, Mass.: Belknap, 2006.

Mao Tse-tung. *Quotations from Chairman Mao Tse-tung*. San Francisco: China Books & Periodicals Inc., 1990.

Mitter, Rana. *A Bitter Revolution: China's Struggle with the Modern World*. New York: Oxford University Press, 2004.

Spence, Jonathan D. *The Search for Modern China*. New York: W.W. Norton & Co., 1999.

FURTHER READING

Ange Zhang. *Red Land Yellow River: A Story from the Cultural Revolution*. Toronto: Groundwood, 2004.

Chun Yu. *Little Green: Growing Up During the Chinese Cultural Revolution*. New York: Simon & Schuster, 2005.

Da Chen. *China's Son: Growing Up in the Cultural Revolution*. New York: Delacorte Press, 2001.

Hatt, Christine. *Mao Zedong*. Milwaukee: World Almanac Library, 2004.

Ji-li Jiang. *Red Scarf Girl: A Memoir of the Cultural Revolution*. Harper Trophy, 1998.

Pietrusza, David. *The Chinese Cultural Revolution*. San Diego: Lucent Books, 1996.

Stewart, Whitney. *Deng Xiaoping: Leader in a Changing China*. Minneapolis: Lerner, 2001.

Index

ABOUT THE AUTHOR

Andrew Langley is the author of many history books for children, including *A Castle at War*, which was shortlisted for the Times Education Supplement Information Book Award. He lives in Wiltshire, England, with his family and two dogs.

IMAGE CREDITS

Corbis/Bettmann **cover** and page 65, akg-images pp. **6** and **42** and **86**, **2** and **45** (Zhou Thong), **30** and **86**; pp. **9**, **11**, **14**, **26**, **34**, **49**, **62–63**, **66**, **69**, **77** (Bettmann), **18** (Archivo Iconografico, S.A.), **32** (Henri Bureau/Sygma), **51**, **59** (Hulton-Deutsch Collection), **72** (Wally McNamee), **82–82** and **88** (Jacques Langevin), **17**; Getty pp. **back cover (left)** and **12** (STF/AP), **back cover (middle)** and **21**, **53**, **71** and **87** (Hulton Archive), **back cover (right)** and 55, **36** and **87** (AFP), **39** (Jean Vincent/AFP), **81** (STR/AFP), **79** and **87**; Shutterstock p. **84** (Michel Stevelmans); Topfoto pp. **61** (World History Archive), **5** and **29** and **86**, **23**.